From the Universe to our Hearts
100 Heartfelt thoughts from the Universe for Everyday Life.

By

Elias Patras

David,
Always
follow your
heart!

Elias Patras

Copyright © 2018 Elias Patras
Liako Publications
All rights reserved.
ISBN-13:
978-1985386693
ISBN-10:
1985386690

DEDICATION

I would like to dedicate this book my parents, who taught me to never give up, that anything is possible. I know that my parents are watching over me and guide me from above along this life path. Because of their love, I am the person who I am today. Thank you, thank you, thank you!

PREFACE

I am always so humbled by the process that happens when I sit down to meditate. I never know what will come to life as I type the words on the computer. I am thrilled to be able to share this process with all of you.

Whether you prefer saying God, Spirit, The Universe, Higher Power, or the Divine, for me I can connect to all of these. It's like saying there are many paths which all go to the same home. I am using the term The Universe with this book, because that is how the information came about. I am so honored to share the words of wisdom from The Universe with all of you. My wish is that these words inspire you, honor you and make you smile.

My hope with the work that I do is to get people to connect to one another on a deeper level and learn from each other so we all can grow.

While having a health issue for 6 months and not able to do physical work, I did a lot of meditation, prayer, and talking to The Universe. Even though I was in physical pain, it forced me to slow down, to go within and to listen. I asked some deep questions and one of the questions was, what is my life purpose.

The answer was simple, to connect other like-minded people by teaching them how to connect to their intuition, their inner voice. This is how The Universe whispers to us.

The simple subtle signs are the things to look for. In doing this we all become educated in hearing those heart-felt thoughts. We all learn in the process, and we grow.

We grow as individuals and as a community. There was the answer. The answer of how to restructure my business and how to put the book in its categories. To Connect, To Educate, To Grow.

ACKNOWLEDGEMENTS

I want to thank all the people that have gone to my workshops, weekend retreat programs, and community college classes. You all are the reason why I continue to do this work. I also want to thank my family, my friends, the group of friends on Facebook, called R-Tribe, thank you all.

A special thanks to Susan Lipshutz, LCSW, of Everyday Medicine Woman who started my journey of self-exploration through indigenous teachings.

My former massage instructors who taught me the connection of the body, mind, spirit.

Thanks to Connie Love of Restore Balance with Love for pushing me to pursue this book and supporting me in all of my business endeavors and being the voice of reason. For being a former instructor, mentor and most importantly dear and close friend.

Thank you to my friend Christine Thom for not only her friendship and love, but for helping me to start to edit this book and for all the encouragement. Thank you for all that you do.

To Moira Scullion, owner of Shungo Healing, for being my partner in crime, co-facilitating our apprenticeship program and supporting me with retreats.

To Gary Gruenewald, a big thank you for starting the retreats with me in the beginning and being my friend through this whole journey.

Joe Kozak, former co-owner of KTK Design, who started my marketing and beginning website designs, for always believing in getting my messages out there. Thank you for being my friend.

Sue Paige of Pathways to Successful Living Seminars. Thank you for helping me to reach my goals, to see the beauty within myself and not to be fearful.

Karla Wetzell of Grama's Healing Porch. Thank you for providing a place for me to grow with my workshops and share the passion of teaching others to connect to their inner voice.

I also want to thank The Universe for so many things. Bringing me into this world, bringing me to my parents, to my family and friends. Having me with wonderful people in my life and helping me to understand, to continue to learn, and to appreciate life and all its mysteries.

HOW TO USE THIS BOOK

I would like to offer a few different suggestions on how to use this book.

1. Take a nice breathe in, and slowly exhale out. When you are relaxed, ask out loud or quietly in your head, what is the lesson for the day. What is it that you are needing to know. Then open to a page.

2. Pick a number 1 thru 100 and open the book to that Heartfelt Thought. That might be the message that you needed to hear for the day.

3. Or take the book in your hands and run thru the pages with your thumb, and when it feels right, stop on that page and read that message.

<u>CONNECT:</u>

Connection is so important on so many levels.
Connecting to self, to others, to nature, to all that is.
When you connect you give the permission of being
open, of saying I care, I am here, and I am present.
~The Universe

1. **CONNECTIONS**.

How do you connect to others? Is it in gesture with a handshake, a pat on the back, or a hug? How do you connect with strangers? Do you get on an elevator and say nothing?

Challenge yourself to see how a simple hello, good morning, or good afternoon would be to people on a bus, train, or elevator.

Sounds silly huh? You never know what a Simple Connection or Random Kindness would do for someone you didn't know.

Spread the love and share the hope.

2. REACHING OUT.

How many times have we given up on things, ideas, or plans?

What do you need to keep yourself on track—to keep you DETERMINED and HOPEFUL?

Share your ideas, your thoughts, fears, frustrations, etc., with someone. Let them support you with what you want to accomplish. Create goals. Have a positive attitude. Don't be afraid to reach out. When we connect with others, we create a community and a "coming together in unity."

3. NEGATIVITY.

Ever been in a funk and it is hard to get out of it? Negative thoughts, patterns, and actions can keep us stuck.

Change that by choosing to do something different: go for a walk, dance, sing out loud, read a good book or grab a movie. Call a friend and tell them you are having a bad day and feel connected with someone.

By doing something positive, you're choosing to change the negative.

4. LAUGH.

Laugh because like attracts like.
Positive feelings bring on more positive feelings.
Be good to yourself.

5. CHOICES.

We all have choices.

The way we choose will affect our day, our plans for the week, our month, and even our lives.

If you choose to eat a huge piece of chocolate cake, you can choose to beat yourself up for it or you can create something positive: eat the cake and then workout and make healthier food choices for the rest of the week.

Loving ourselves is something we don't always do, but it's a choice that we have to improve our day.

6. TIME OUT.

So many of us do so much for others. So many of us don't take time to do for ourselves.

How can you "TREAT" yourself today? Take yourself out for a YOU DATE.

Spend some time in nature, grab some coffee or your favorite drink, and spend at least 15-30 minutes in your own company just to reboot yourself.

Just be with yourself for that time. Enjoy taking the time out by enjoying what is around you and your own company.

Experience the unwinding of the chaos of the day.

Taking time out for you is a wonderful way to SELF LOVE.

7. PASSION.

What are you passionate about? What gets you so excited that you can't contain yourself? Are you passionate about what you are doing with your life?

Ever look someone in the eye and see that there is a glow within them or around them? Or that there is a lightness about them when they walk?

This week, ignite your passion from within. Share your passion, or your pursuit of your passion, and inspire others to do the same.

Not sure what your passion is? Get out there and try things and see what moves you. Sometimes we are afraid to try, but then we only stay stuck. Show the world what you are made of—move mountains—and build your dreams.

All it takes is getting into the mindset of feeling your desire and going for it.

8. KINDNESS.

Share random acts of kindness. See how they can changed your day. Just by smiling at someone or buying the person behind you a cup of coffee, or a compliment to someone can just change their day.
When you give you also receive, what a joy it is to receive.
Challenge yourself with random acts of kindness and see what comes back in return when you are not looking for it.
Kindness radiates within and can crack open the mold that we can be stuck in.

9. HONOR.

What do you honor the most? Who do you honor? Have you told them? Do you honor yourself? What can you do to honor yourself? Do you constantly give to others and forget about yourself? Do you honor your work time?

Know that sometimes there are days that we may not fully honor and celebrate ourselves. There may have been days when we allowed ourselves to only feel complete by others.

Treasure the relationships that you have had and continue to have. Honor each thing that you do, each person that comes in your life, even if they come into your life just for the day. Honor your pets for they are our silent teachers. Be grateful for others that have come into your life.

Honor the beauty of each day, each moment.

10.   SELF.

When you wake up in the morning and look in the mirror what do you see? Love, Kindness, Beauty, Happiness? Frustration, Bitterness, Sadness?

Do you decide that you are going to put a mask on for others to see who you are or who you want to be or who they want you to be?

Leave the mask at home and let the gratitude of who you are and who you inspire to be rest within you.

A smile can change a person's day, including your own.

11. **LISTEN**.

Just for a few minutes take time to listen.
Listen to nature.
Listen to your inner voice.
Listen to the person sitting across or next
to you without interrupting them.
Take time to slow down and just listen.
Find the treasure in just being still.

12.   **SMILE**.

What makes you smile from your heart?
Walking your dogs and watching them
wag their tails? Seeing a baby smiling or
laughing? Seeing an old couple holding
hands?
Share your smile and smile back at them.
Smile and say to all that you meet, have a
nice day.
What a blessing a smile is.
See how the Universe smiles back. Maybe
something in nature catches your eye?
Or while you're walking you see a white
butterfly following you and you smile.
Share the smile today; we all need them.

13.   HAPPINESS.

What makes you happy? Cooking a favorite meal, going out to a restaurant, hearing a favorite song, reading, or just having some down time?

Whatever it is, do something HAPPY for at least 30 minutes today. See how that 30 minutes can be done every day and soon that turns into an hour, then make a whole day of it.

Enjoy being HAPPY and take someone along for the ride.

Share the WEALTH.

## 14.	EXPRESS.

Express yourself openly, honestly, and from the heart.
See what gift is given and also received when you do.

15. **INTUITION**.

We all have it; we use it without even knowing it.

It's that gut feeling about something, it's when you just "know" that you are doing the right thing.

It's usually the first thought that you get about something and then your brain kicks in and dismisses it.

Trust, Honor, Feel, and GROW your intuition.

Connecting to your intuition is truly trusting yourself.

Start today just by going with what you FEEL and see what happens.

This is how The Universe talks to us by whispering into our hearts, into our inner voice, where intuition is stored.

16.   STOP!

Just for a moment STOP and listen to what others are truly saying.

Look at their body language. Look and see if their words and body are saying the same thing.

STOP and listen to your own words. Do they match your actions?

STOP and listen to your heartbeat, does it get excited when you see someone you care about, or watch a movie, or see someone smile.

Just for today, STOP and smell the roses. Everyone is rushing around and not paying enough attention to others and even their own actions, words and thoughts.

STOP, SMILE, and have GRATITUDE.

17.   LISTEN.

Take time today to listen.
Listen to your own words.
Listen to the words of others.
Listen to the silence.
Listen to the wind blow.
See what happens today when you actually
LISTEN.
See what happens when you fully listen to
a person instead of cutting them off.
Look in their eyes and just listen.
The observation of this could be very life
changing.

18.   SMILE.

This is a very simple and easy thing to do but also can be a challenge. We have no problem smiling to those we know.

How about SMILING at the cashier at Starbucks or at the Grocery Store.

SMILING when you walk into an elevator and saying good morning as everyone else is so quiet. Spice it up today!!!

Smile for a reason, or for no reason at all.

You never know how contagious a smile and kindness can be.

19.   **ALL IS GOOD**.

There are days when we take things for granted. There are days when we think that all is lost, and we can start letting ourselves get into a downward spiral.

STOP. BREATHE. SAY THANK YOU.

Notice the small things in life and the joy that it gives you. Perhaps you have seen a night's snowfall, how SWEET and MAGICAL it can be. The snow glistening in the light making it a very different kind of snow, like shimmering white glitter. You can see all its wonder. A camera couldn't capture its beauty. In that moment, ALL IS GOOD!!! The chaos of the day, the OH NO's and the frustration just stopped.

In that observation of whatever you observe as magical, you can feel you have a great life. In that moment recognize that we all can get stuck in the craziness of worry and regret or we can STOP, BREATHE and say THANK YOU and honor the gifts, the joys, and the wonderment that we have in our lives.

Most importantly acknowledging THE MORE of all those things that are coming BECAUSE of that particular moment.

Take some time today to honor ALL IS GOOD.

20.   **STILLNESS**.

It's interesting to notice what happens when you turn off the cell phone, the TV, the computer and allow yourself to BE STILL from the ways we spend filling up our time. Give yourself at least one hour a day to yourself with no distractions.
Listen to music, take a walk, journal, or read a book.
Give yourself some great DOWN TIME.
It's amazing to see what you can find out about yourself in an hour.

21. **HUMOR**.

Can you find the joy of laughing?
When you laugh, it changes your whole
energy. It sends messages and chemicals
to the brain and shifts your mood.
Go out and see a funny movie, share a
funny joke, or just go be silly and enjoy
yourself.

22.   **POSITIVE CHALLENGES**.

Challenge yourself with changing your frame of mind.

Do you say: "I wish I had more money; I want better health; I want a good relationship." Why aren't I finding someone?

Change the energy of what you say for the next 30 days.

For example, instead of saying I want more money, try saying I am increasing my income every single day.

If you say, "Ugh I am so overweight, I hate my body". Try, I am improving my body every single day in every way.

Say it until you make it.

The words form a change in attitude and in energy. You will start noticing little things shifting by the end of the month.

Take the challenge.

Say something like, I love me and everything I do increases my prosperity and abundance.

23.   **CONNECTION TO SELF**.

How do we connect to ourselves? When was the last time you took a walk by a lake or rode a bike or did something by yourself that was for yourself with no distractions?

Connecting to oneself, even for 5 minutes, without distractions, recharges the body, mind, and spirit. It's like an energetic boost that you want to share with another.

24.   **CONNECTION TO OTHERS**.

When was the last time you actually picked up the phone to call someone that you have only chatted with via text? When was the last time you sent them a card via the postal service to say thank you, or just thinking about you?
By connecting to others in a heartfelt way allows us to connect on a deeper level.

25.   **THANKFUL**.

Be mindful of the small things that you take for granted and be thankful for them. If it is the bagger at the grocery store who always smiles and says thank you and means it, let them know their smile makes your day.

If it's a baby's laugh on the train, tell the parent, what a great laugh your child has. Or just waking up this morning and seeing the sun beaming through your window. Take a moment and be grateful and thankful that today will be a better day than yesterday.

Call or message someone that you haven't chatted with in a long time, but you are glad that they are part of your life.

Whatever it may be, share the thought with yourself or another and be THANKFUL.

26.   **GENTLE SURPRISES**.

Those are the subtle things that can happen during the day.
A baby's smile that makes you smile.
An animal that wags their tail.
A phone call from a friend that you haven't heard from.
A glance from a person from across the room that catches your eye.
Anything that warms your heart and puts a smile on your face.
Those wonderful things can Surprise you and make you feel special.
Surprise someone today, put a smile on their face.

27.   **INSPIRATION**.

Who and what inspires you?
If it is someone, let them know.
Inspire others with your inspiration.

28.   HUGS.

We need to give and receive them.
Hugs allow a physical and emotional connection.
Its good when we show we care with a hug.

29.   HAPPINESS.

The feeling that you get when you are greeted by a smile, a warm embrace, or spending time with people that you connect with.

Share a smile and embrace or a kind gesture with someone today.

Your small gift of kindness might make their day.

30.   LOVE YOURSELF.

Love you with all your perfections and imperfections. That is what makes you unique.

Love the bumps, rolls, dimples and freckles.

If you are looking for love, love yourself first.

By loving yourself, you radiate that love from the inside out. This sends out an unseen signal of worthiness, confidence and of, I DESERVE the love.

Ask for THE ONE to be put into your life. The one who truly loves you will love all of you for just being you. Your True Unique Self.

31. TIME.

It allows us to collect our thoughts and feelings.
It also allows us to be able to communicate them clearly.
When the time is right, the words come easily.

32. WHO YOU REALLY ARE.

Ever feel like you are wearing a mask?
Showing others what they want to see
instead of where you truly are?
Honor your feelings. It's okay to admit the
truth and be truly honest with yourself.
Be authentic and be you!
If you find you are in a negative space,
then admit it and slowly accept where you
are in that moment.
When you reveal the "True You,"
everything begins to feel lighter and
easier, and you slowly begin to have this
warm feeling in your heart. This feeling
then allows you to start feeling happier.
When we feel better, it's really easy to let
the true you shine through.
When you take the mask off you lighten
up and reveal the true you to the world.

33. GIVING UP.

You can give up on bad habits, poor diet, judging others, being closed minded, but NEVER GIVE UP on yourself or the help of others.
Sometimes we all need support.
One kind word can make A LOT of difference.

34.   **HEART TO HEART.**

Believe in yourself and see the beauty that you are in true form.
One heart touches another.

35.   TIME.

Small miracles happen to everyone each day. No matter what tradition you come from, what you follow, they all teach to give of yourself.
Make small miracles happen to someone by giving of yourself.
Time is the most precious thing.
Your action can make a difference in someone's life with your time.

36.   TIME.

Take an extra moment to ask someone
how they are doing.
When asked, how are you doing, usually
the response is "Fine, or Ok".
Take that extra time to reach out and
REALLY ask how they are feeling.
You could bring a smile to someone's face
just by letting them know that you
REALLY care.

37.   AN IDEA.

Take a look at all your Facebook friends.
Pick one to three people that you have not
talked to in a long time, call them.
If you don't have their phone number, ask
for it.
Who knows, the ones that you have chosen
to call probably needed to hear a message
from you.

38.   **ASK.**

Don't be afraid to ask for what you need, you may be pleasantly surprised.

39.   INSPIRE.

When we are feeling good about ourselves
it becomes contagious.
Inspire others with your own inspiration.

40. TAKE A CHANCE.

Take a chance to get to know someone on a deeper level, not just superficially. Watch the wonderful bond that can happen.

EDUCATE:

To educate is all about learning and sharing. When educating self, it gives the opportunity to educate others. Within that process we learn something more about ourselves and one another.
~The Universe

41.   **REGRETS**.

We all have our "should of", "could have,"
and "would have" moments.
If we keep beating ourselves up about
them, we can't move forward.
Acknowledge the past, be present now,
and then allow yourself to move forward.
All of these may look hard, but once you
take the first step, the rest is easy.

42.　　**BELIEVE YOU CAN DO
ANYTHING**.

Things get hard, and we all have made
excuses for the "Why I can't accomplish
one thing or another."
But believing in oneself is the MOST
important thing for being able to do
whatever your heart is leading you to do.

43.   **TIME**.

Honor it, savor it, love it.
There is a structured around it: time to get up and time to rest.
We might say "I'll do that next time," "Maybe another time," or "Who has time for that?"
It's about taking our TIME.
Be in the moment.
Take the time to do things that make you happy.
Thank others for their time.
Take the time to reach out and to reach within.
Share your time with others.

44.   FEAR.

What holds us back from what we want?
It's our Fear.
Fear of what people will think.
Fear of not being good enough.
Fear of being wrong.
What can we replace it with?
Confidence? Love? Patience? Taking a Chance? All of these things.
Take a chance and go for what you want and feel good about what you are doing. If it doesn't work, at least you know that that particular way doesn't work.
Keep going. Go for what you want.
See the light at the end of the tunnel.

45.   **GRATITUDE**.

What are you grateful for today?
This moment? This week?
We can sometimes focus on the "Don't haves" instead of the "Do haves."
So, each morning when you get up, be grateful for the things that you have in your life: "I am grateful for the abundant love and support I receive from all the people in my life".
Enjoy the little things and the big things in life.
An attitude of gratitude can bring in more good energy.

46.   RENEWAL.

The Spring season can be a time of rebirth, renewal, and for recreating what you truly want.

The Universe would like to invite you to feel that each day.

Each moment can be a chance to turn over a new leaf, to reboot ourselves. Think of it as an opportunity to start with improved focus and motivation.

RENEW yourself from the inside out and see how it will inspire others.

47.   THINGS HAPPEN.

Sometimes we might not understand why things happen.
If you can believe that things always happen for a reason, you have already started to see and feel the shift in your personal journey.
This shift leads you to another step forward, and then another step. Your problem is not the problem, it can be the start of the solution to where you need to go next.
Embrace your inner strength.
You got this and The Universe supports you.

48. **OPPORTUNITY**.

Sometimes we can be afraid to go for what we want.
Sometimes when we have blinders on we can't see what options we have.
Know that when opportunity knocks, we need to answer.
The Universe has your back.

49.   ACTION.

What is it that you want to do? What is it that you want?

To get IT (whatever IT is), we have to step up into ACTION.

It's a simple ASK for what you want (put it out to the Universe), SEE (it coming to you), give THANKS (thank it for coming as if it has already come to you), and LET GO OF THE OUTCOME.

If it isn't coming, then you are bound to get something better than what you asked for.

Taking Action starts the Universe hearing your call and your willingness to receive.

50.   **EXPAND**.

What would it be like if we could expand our minds and take a chance on thinking outside of the box?

How do we limit ourselves by the way we think?

Do we even truly take in another person's opinion?

Do something different today: be LIMITLESS.

Take a chance to really spread your wings, have faith, and see yourself taking flight!!!

You automatically do this by thinking outside of the box by expanding your thoughts, feelings and expressing yourself.

51. PROGRESS.

Love the progress that you make.
Even if it is a baby step.
You didn't bite your nails today.
You had half a slice of cake instead of the whole piece.
You told your significant other that you needed to walk away for 10 minutes before blowing up.
Each step is a progression of where you used to be.
Each step gets you to where you want to be.

52.   ASSUMPTIONS.

How many of us have thought of something but found out that it wasn't true, it was just an assumption.
By letting go of the assumptions and being open and honest with questions, it takes away all the what we thought or felt and allows us to be in TRUTH.

53.   IMAGINE.

Whatever you imagine can come true if you let go of fear and doubt.
Look deep in your mind and heart; see what you want and GO FOR IT.
Don't let anything get in your way. You DESERVE it!!!
Whatever you IMAGINE can make your life feel and be brand new.

54.   **CONSCIOUSNESS**.

Start each day out with being conscious of your thoughts, actions, and words.
Be mindful and listen/speak from the heart.
Your words/actions not only affect others but also affect you.
Saying something like, I am so stupid, I am so poor, or I am ugly, is hurtful to ourselves and to others.
Reflect what is truly in the inside and let that light and energy shine outward.
I am loved.
I am abundant.
I am smart.
The I AM, affects everyone around you.

55.   ANIMAL GUIDES.

Many things or people can come to us as guides. People in our lives can be mentors; they can inspire us and teach us so much. In many Indigenous traditions animals are guides as well.

What animal do you like to see at the zoo? What animals interest you?

Find out what their spiritual message is online. See what lessons or teachings they have for you.

Each thing of Nature can give us much information.

Our lessons and teachings come in many forms.

56.   THE WHY.

Did you ever wonder WHY when you are stuck in life?

Sometimes the WHY happens so that you can get to the OH and then to the AH HA. Our challenges take us on a path that helps us become stronger to then be able to give to someone else who might be in the WHY and we can then help them along to the OH.

Everything always happens for a reason. Be kind to yourself and enjoy the ride on the path.

57.   **VULNERABILITY.**

Take a moment to have courage to be able to open yourself up and be seen.
Some may judge, and some may not, but to know that you are being authentic is a gift to yourself.
Standing in that moment and being vulnerable with an open heart and open mind might just inspire others to do the same.

58.   SUCCESS.

What measures Success?
Is it money? Power? Popularity?
By following your heart and your dreams
that is what measures true success.
Focus on how you feel, what moves and
inspires you.
Go within, listen, feel, dream, and make it
happen. THAT is finding your success. It
has always been within you.
You were born that way.

59.   TRUST.

Trust that you are where you need to be right here and right now.
Trust that each day allows you an opportunity for growth, as we grow we help others to grow.
Set an example.
Trust that the best decision is being made for you for your highest good.
Trust in yourself to believe that your heart can open even wider and you will be safe.

60. EXPECTATIONS.

Be true to yourself and expect great things of yourself.
When you open your mind to the limitless possibilities of what The Universe has in mind for you, amazing things can happen.

61.   **WORDS.**

Be mindful of what you say and how it is said.
Words and the emotion behind them can affect not only others but you as well.
Before you react verbally, take a breath, check in with yourself, and speak from your heart place.
Trust that the correct words will come out.

62.   TRUST.

Trust is earned, but we have to earn it for ourselves first.

Trust that you are doing what you need to be doing right at this moment.

If you follow your heart's path, you will be in the right place.

Even if you stray for a bit, perhaps that lesson is what you needed to have stronger trust and faith in yourself.

63.   THE UNIVERSE.

What would it feel like if you heard, I
believe in you.
How would that one sentence change your
vision, your goal, your outlook?
The Universe believes in you.
Trust This, Know This, Own This.

64.   BELIEVE.

Opportunity is always out there.
The key is to find out how to get rid of the obstacles that get in our way.
Be able to make yourself fully available by believing, truly believing, in you.

65. FAITH.

Have faith to go out on a limb and stand out in the crowd; you will find that you are not alone.

66.   LET GO.

Just for today, take a moment to see what is holding you back.

Where do you feel stuck?

Is it the not knowing the unknown?

Is it the feeling of not getting what you want?

What is one thing that you can do to shift that?

By LETTING GO of the negative thoughts and despair, the feeling of gratitude for what you do know, want, and have can rush in and change things in an instant.

67.   **FRUSTRATION.**

How do you deal with it? Do you get angry, cry, avoid others, or yell? Some of us may get frustrated and reach the point of anger and get mad at ourselves that we couldn't deal with it differently. We might even punish ourselves by eating our emotions or some other sort of self-sabotage.

Instead of putting yourself in a bad place, tell the other person that you are getting frustrated, and how it's making you feel at that moment. Tell them you would like to discuss taking a "time out" and then come back to the situation. When we come back to a space where we can focus and speak from the heart, our problems and concerns can be heard. We then we can move forward. Remember to thank the person or the situation for listening.

When we can share, we can grow.

68.   **TODAY.**

It is a new day.
It is the opportunity to start new, to do something different, to learn from yesterday and create what you really want. Even if you are reading this in the afternoon or evening.
You still can create something new, something different.
Be in the moment. Because each moment brings new ideas, new inspirations.
Isn't it about time we stop focusing on beating ourselves up and do something about it?

<u>GROW</u>

Growth is so important. Without growth there is stagnation. There is no movement there is no fluidity. To inspire one another is giving that gift of expansion. It is a beautiful gift that you can give. This allows you to step out of the box and truly see the vastness of your own possible expansion. When you grow and inspire, you then touch the lives of others.
~The Universe

69.   **PATIENCE**.

Have you ever been upset at the person in the car who cut you off while driving?

Have you gotten frustrated with the sales person who didn't answer your question fast enough? Or have you ever been frustrated by your friends because they didn't understand you or didn't pay attention to you?

Put yourself in their shoes for a minute. It could have been that the person who cut you off was in a rush to go somewhere because of an emergency. The sales person didn't know the answer to your question and had to think about it for a minute. And your friend was so preoccupied about a challenge that happened in their life that they were not present in that moment.

We never know what someone is really going through unless we ask.

Take a moment, breathe, relax, and have patience with others.

Wouldn't you want the same compassion and patience given to you?

70.   **TRUE YOU**.

Are you being true to yourself?
Do you wear a mask showing the world one attitude when you really are feeling another?
Honor your feelings. It's okay to admit the truth and be truly honest with yourself. Be authentic and be you! Even if you happen to be in a negative space, admit it and slowly accept where you are in this moment. When you reveal the "True You," everything begins to feel lighter and easier; you'll slowly begin to have a warm feeling in your heart, and you'll start feeling happier. When you take the mask off, you lighten up and reveal the true you to the Universe. Let yourself SHINE, the Universe is waiting.

71.   **CREATE**.

Create by visualizing the things that you want.

To manifest those things, see yourself having them, or see yourself being that person that you want to be.

Actually, SEE IT—imagine it as vividly as you can each and every day.

When that happiness or something similar within, it radiates and attracts the things that you want.

Manifesting is not only about envisioning what you want, it's about knowing that you deserve to be the person you want to be and to have the things you wish to have.

The only thing in the way is Fear.

72.   **LUCK**.

Think of all those things that make you lucky.

What brings you luck?

Is it a lucky charm or habit?

A positive attitude that you create each day?

Here's an idea...Notice when you are being more positive, it can bring a sense of happiness. This can then can have a sense of feeling like more luck is in your life.

By manifesting what you want, you can have a sense of feeling lucky because great things are happening to you.

73.   **PERSISTENCE**.

Ever feel stuck and think that you can't push through?
Then, from some unknown place, you find the will to stick with it or give it another go?
It's such a great feeling when you've pushed through to the other side of the situation!
Remember that feeling the next time you feel stuck. Don't settle; push through.
Speak up, Be Present, Believe in You!!!

74.   **AWARENESS.**

Take time to sit and actually notice the flowers bloom, listen to the birds, feel the wind, your heartbeat.
In this stillness of awareness many thoughts or revelations can occur.
Like the old saying goes, if you want someone's attention, whisper so they have to listen.
When we stop to listen, observe, hear, we get inspired, we can share, and grow.

75.   **OPPORTUNITY**.

Did you ever wonder what stops us from an OPPORTUNITY and allows us to stay stuck?

In most cases, the answer is FEAR.

Fear of success, fear of failure, fear of looking silly, fear of (fill in the blank).

Take a chance and take the opportunity to watch your wings expand.

Trust that you have the inner knowing to succeed.

Watch yourself soar.

76.   PERFECTION.

Did you ever feel that things have to be perfect?

"If it's not perfect, it's not right; if it's not right, then I'm not right, and what will others think?"

The Universe gives us a gift of learning, of being ok with our imperfections.

In this beautiful way, we get to discover ourselves.

Let go and just be!!!

Sometimes the "being perfect" is what gets in our way of discovery.

77.   **CONFIDENCE**.

May you always follow what your heart is saying, regardless of what other people may think of you.

78. PERSEVERANCE.

We can find that even though it can be tough, moving forward gets us to where we want to be.

Also, recognize that stopping and taking a moment to re-evaluate is taking time to continue to move forward.

Don't think of it as just standing still.

On the contrary, it's having the forward action to getting the goal.

Having the perseverance allows us to love the journey!

79.   **ACCOMPLISHMENTS.**

Take time today to acknowledge your accomplishments.
They don't have to be big ones.
Even if you lost a pound this week, that is an accomplishment.
Don't squelch it by saying, "it's only a pound".
If you were able to make someone laugh or smile today, know that it's coming from the gift that you have within you.
Take time to ACKNOWLEDGE every step that you take.
Each step forward is a BIG STEP.

80.   PATTERNS.

Many of us do the same thing every day. We talk about how we can or will change things, then continue to go back to our old pattern because it's what we know and are comfortable in.

CHANGE is difficult.

It takes courage, strength, and a leap of faith to do something different.

Instead of talking about doing something different, JUST DO IT and BE IT.

Make the commitment and take action.

Believing in self, honoring self, and loving self truly is about GROWTH.

Break old patterns.

See the huge E X P A N S I O N and the possibilities that you will have.

81.   LAUGHTER.

Laughing is truly the best medicine.
When you laugh, your laughter can make
someone else laugh and you could laugh
harder because of it.
Laughter is good for the soul.
Laugh and smile today, just because.
See how that will change your day and
how it inspires others to do the same.

82.   **REFLECTION.**

Take a good look at yourself today.
Remind yourself of all the awesome
accomplishments that you have done.
Remind yourself of all the possibilities that
you have made because of your hard work.
Take time today to pat yourself on the
back, even for the small things.
Isn't that easier than sitting in the should
have, could have, would have place?
Look in the mirror, smile and love yourself
more, just for today.
And tomorrow, love yourself even more.

83. FEELING STUCK.

Sometimes we can get in a rut about things, feel ourselves spiral and reach a place of being in a rut.
Maybe that rut allows a time of gathering info, introspection, a time to reflect.
Its ok to honor those feelings and then focus on the things that we have in our lives that we value.
Take time to feel what you need but move thru those things, seek support from others, reach out, don't hide for too long.
We are all a beacon of light, that needs to shine.

84.   CURIOSITY.

What are you curious about?
Is it about a new hobby, a book, or a
person?
Take the next step to reach out and ask
questions or just go do.
If you are curious about something and
don't try it, you will never know if it could
lead you to what you are wanting.
So, go ice-skating for the first time, read a
different kind of book, ask the new kid in
class or the new person on the job to lunch
to find out more about them.
See what wonders will come to you when
you reach out and reach within.

85.   **CELEBRATE UNDERSTANDING**.

Did you ever have a disagreement that you regretted acting out?

Did you have a "conditional" way that you have reacted to a topic or person?

Have you CHOSEN recently to react differently?

If so CELEBRATE that newfound UNDERSTANDING, no matter how big or small.

Making a shift or a change is allowing you to see things differently.

Congratulations on a new page or a new chapter of you!

86.   **REFLECTION**.

Have you ever noticed that the people who come into your life often mirror you? Sometimes this can be wonderful and loving, and sometimes a bit challenging. There might be something about that person that annoys you or frustrates you. Take a look within and see what they are doing REFLECTS yourself.

Or perhaps there is something that you are just realizing, and you have that AHA moment and can share your experience with them.

Whatever the case, honor that REFLECTION. Treasure it!!!

That mirror is there to help you grow. Who you are really reflects on the outside. Be that AMAZING person that you are.

87. TAKING ACTION.

How many times do we say, "I have to exercise," but we spend the day on the couch? Or we say that we have to call the friend we haven't talked to in a long time, yet and the day goes by and we didn't call them. Or we say that we should really volunteer somewhere, etc.

These things can start to pile up and we can beat ourselves up about more things that we didn't do.

Change that by Making a to-do list—not a mental one, but an actual list. Make it realistic.

As you start to do things and cross them off the list, you will find out that there are going to be wonderful things that start coming back to you. This is because you made room in your life by letting go of the "should of, could of, would of"pile.

Take Action and see how you expand your possibilities!!!

88.   **FORGIVENESS**.

Forgiveness of self, others, and assumption.

When we let go and allow ourselves to forgive past wounds, we allow growth.

It doesn't matter whether the wounds were caused by others or by our own selves; letting go allows deeper healing.

When we hold onto wounds, we often tend to scrape at the emotional scab, which can cause the original wound to become larger. Then we are left with that much more to heal. Forgive, and express that forgiveness to yourself and to others.

There is power in letting old wounds go. Watch what happens.

89. **TOLERANCE**.

When we are sitting in a room, bus, train, or at a party, are we tolerant of others? Or are we quick to judge, assume, or put someone in a box of how we think they are or what their story is?
We are all different, and we all have unique gifts.
If we take time to ask questions and look into ourselves, we may be more tolerant and more important and have more PATIENCE with others.

90.   POSSIBILITIES.

Take a look at where you were a few months ago, a year ago, even a few days ago.
YOU are able to make anything possible by allowing yourself to dream. Set a goal and not give up on it—move through and attain it—anything is truly possible. Whatever the accomplishment is, no matter how big or small, give yourself a pat on the back there isn't anything we can't do when we put our Minds and Hearts into it.

91.   CROSSROADS.

Ever come to the middle of the road and
you have two paths that you can take?
If you go one way will you regret not
taking the other path?
Trust that you will make the right decision,
for in that moment, it is the right decision.
It will lead you to where you need to be.
Trust and Believe in Knowing.

92.   ACCEPTANCE.

When we learn to accept ourselves for who we are, the good, the bad and the ugly, we can truly accept the beauty of others that are put in our path for a reason.
That is the journey of self-acceptance.
Love yourself!
For you are the best you, right now and in this moment.

93.   BEAUTY.

If beauty is in the eye of the beholder, take a good look at yourself in the mirror and see how beautiful you are.

Beauty is not just on the outside.

WHO YOU ARE on the inside, makes you OUTSTANDING.

Take a good look and see what others who love you see: your inner beauty makes you radiant.

94.   **DECISIONS**.

Take a moment, breathe, and listen to what your heart wants.
Take the leap of faith and move with it, it's a growth experience.

95.   RECOGNITION.

Honor yourself today by recognizing all that you have done for yourself.
Then RECOGNIZE and HONOR those who have helped you to this point and their journey.

## 96.	SURRENDER.

Let go of what you think should happen. When you allow the process to unfold, it can bring you much more than you originally thought.

97.　SPEAKING FROM THE HEART.

When you speak from the heart there are no regrets.
Why hold onto so much over thinking with our brains.
Remember your heart is valuable and strong; believe in yourself and watch what will happen.

98.   **AFFIRMATION.**

When things look really doubtful, that's when you have to believe, trust, and acknowledge your own inner strength.
Write a positive affirmation.
Let go of the reigns and see what the possibilities are in store for you.

99.   CLARITY.

Clarity comes to us if we are open to listening to it, by slowing down. Breathe, Believe, Trust, and Thanks.

100.   ASK.

Don't be afraid to ask for what you want, you may be pleasantly surprised.

ABOUT THE AUTHOR

Elias Patras was born in Athens, Greece and adopted by Greek-Americans. His parents were 46 and 56 years old when they adopted him. They taught him to never give up on his dreams. He remembers his Mom saying to him, "If we took no for an answer, or didn't believe we could adopt a child, you wouldn't be here with us, today". Elias grew up in Chicago for his early years and moved to a Chicago suburb for his teen years and then back to Chicago. He studied psychology and communication and has always been fascinated by the psychological and spiritual connection. He continues to facilitate retreats and workshops in person and online, as well as working with clients privately. He is currently working on his second book. He resides with his 2 dogs, Harry and Willow, in Sterling, Illinois.

Follow Elias Patras on
Facebook @ www.Facebook.com/EliasPatras/
You Tube
And his website www.EliasPatras.com

Made in the USA
Middletown, DE
30 September 2021

48866135R00130